Mischievous Spurtle

Jim McRobert

To my friends
Irene + Stewart
Jim

ISBN 978-1-78222-989-6

Book design, layout and production management by Into Print
www.intoprint.net
+44 (0)1604 832149

CONTENTS

I dedicate this book

to seekers of the Truth, Integrity and Sincerity worldwide
many of whom have died in their search.

Acknowledgements

I'd like to thank my friend Charlie Fraser for keeping my rhymes in rein; my partner Sue Leiper for proof-reading, editing and specially her drive to get me to publish this; David Hamilton for drawings; Michelle Elliot, Eleanore Hunter, Charlotte Shyllon, Campbeltown Courier for support and friends and family who have helped me through the trauma of publication.

RWANDAN MAN

It was Mai-Mai that gave me pain
murdered all my family to steal a hand of grain
started me on this journey
will it never end?
Running from their bullets with wounds that cease to mend
Fear my diet constant to run or hide by chance
No more the stirring drum-beat or stories in our dance
Each step a run through Africa, twitch when offered meat
Living in the shadows survive by cheat to eat

Caught I've slaved for pittance, escaped as threat appeared
fought with thirst in desert; each city, town I feared

Kagame is hunting, he targets all I hear
Some have died in foreign lands behind me lurks a spear
Thirty years of running this Rwandan man's escape
the wildest things that men can do torture, beatings, rape
Trapped for years in Borders while tyrants shuffle cards
welcoming the wealthy us Poor their system bars

Once I paddled No-Man's-Land prayed they'd let me stay
now shackled to a Border Guard as they send me far away

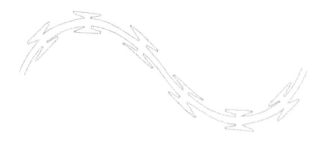

EXPENDABLES?

Would you swim in a cemetery among the bones of the dead
No thought of children going over your head
ignore all their screams you in your seaside swim
at the waters of the Med

You who eat at the restaurants never a thought for the fish
of skin and flesh it ate there in your favourite dish
Maybe you worry about plastic that's tragic but naught compared to a child
Ghoul-like ghost float on a sun-lit coast its waters tainted, defiled

Would you laugh in the face of adversity in your land of no escape
willing to stand in front of the guns to eat up its pieces of eight
or fly through the gates of Hell each step a tentative hope
Trust in the good of fellow Man to be used like like a turd of soap

What is this to do with me you may ask as My daughter floats in the Med
Fifty crammed in a hustlers boat Forty-nine of those folk dead
Each one in need to escape the stranglehold of Man
and I prayed that you had a bit of guilt but you couldn't care a damn!

Forced upon a smugglers' boat with no one there to tell
know not where they're going but sure it must be Hell
But I survived and begged someone hear my cry
Ignored as vagrant where I lie in your playground lullaby

ONCE WE WERE PEOPLE

We've been smuggled into Everyland
Mule-train from everywhere and France
Stolen as innocents
to do the Slavers dance

Some travelled for improvement
Now trapped in No-Man's-Land
Bait to feed an evil trade
but cannot make a stand

We're dying by the thousand
yet every Country's curse
Pariah seen as lowest caste
puts wealth to gangsters' purse

No one hears our suffering
We're dumb; but with a need
as slaves or future body parts
Please, someone hear us plead!

PARIAHS IN POWER

They're removing the dirt from Society they say
The stuff that they see as pure trash
Plastic and sewage and people
Dumped while many think rash
Propping up dictators and bullies
in countries that'll do as they're bid
While washing their hands of murder
despite every action they did

Windrush was such an occasion
to please all their friends on the Right
Now it's survivors of battles and drownings
given Passport to die as their blight
These Pariahs call themselves Christian
The Right thing to do they all say
Done by the sleight hand of Brexit
Here's hoping their future is grey

REFUGEE

I'm a runner not sportsman for me it's no game,
stealing for privilege states political claim
I live in the shadows not seen but by few
grubbing by night in each trash-bin queue

I'm a runner from Africa or Afghanistan
Syrian, Palestinian or Yemeni man
No escapee from prison I'm living my time
Tabled as parasite to exist is a crime

I'm a runner with fear; a dread of the past
Stepping each pace, distances vast
Starvation, thirst, exhaustion; what?
Crossing deserts ice-cold, some hot

I'm a runner from sex-gangs who'd maim for a thrill
Slave of the brothels; prostitutes they'd kill
Fearing the extremist, God trapped in their head
Shirking, secretive; democracy's dead

I'm not a runner to learning, I speak many tongues
Educated in survival, I've climbed all the rungs
Worth a great fortune if I'd just find my place
Yet no chance of that when not allowed in the race

I'm a Runner no Greyhound, Terrier or Poodle
Never treated to treats cuddles or canoodle
one of the family yet led like a slave
My place in society; with no stone for my grave

AMERICA'S BLACK MARK

Let's compare German and American big business
through the eyes of a good microscope
during World War two they were hidden from view to deny peoples a hope
In Germany it all came to the surface by who ever survived their Hell
for these people were literate of the cruelty and treatment they'd tell

In America it was the abuse of the Black man, a plague on the Rights of free men
stolen by the rich and powerful; herded like pigs in a pen
The North had fought to stop Slavery something soon forgot by the South
Education to black folks a secret; repression by lethal white mouth

Judges sold free men as convicts to work deep in the mines
or leased each to farmers, despite never doing a crime
More than 100,000 were used in the Steel Mills; thousands picked Cotton on farms
creating free labour for the greedy; shearing the fleece off these lambs

"Mr President, they won't let me have him since they've locked my boy in chains
so I pleading to you Mr President my poor boy was never to blame"
Then as now her pleading was wasted, her son would never be found
trapped digging coal for a magnate his body lying deep underground

There's a depression in the ground before me, buttons and teeth scattered round
It's the graveyard of many poor black men, where Slaves to this Steelyard are found
Few of the white folks objected, said 'They deserved everything that they got'
It was known the Black man was lazy, Abolition was quickly forgot

BERLIN WALL – A DIVISION

I wasn't there when the Wall came down
Such tears of joy that I might drown
Relief, hope; new-sense loss
Elated heart from unburdened Cross
Yet heard the tales astride on Wall
Betwixt the rage destroy, destroy
Cleanse that place; scour its dust
No more policed by evil lust

Remove each Mine; all Razor Wire
Topple towers by freedom fire
Let us unite all East and West
Right past wrongs to be the Best

A year gone by almost two
aliens to them; could be true
Second class we piece of shit
beneath their heel is where we sit
Useless toys trapped in cage
by those our neighbours
who refuse to change!!

A ROCK TO PERISH ON

I'm a Benefit cheat, a liar
Yes, this society's sick pariah
and I can't raise a hand in my defence
Since this Government's created issue
now blames us poor, in any situ
cause they've lost any case-notes to reference

When an injury at work
brought me face to face with luck
and I trusted in the honesty of facts
But now they say I'm lazy
not their Health Service is crazy
for failing in a service that it lacks

I'm just a single feller
I told the lady teller
don't support any family or my Mum
Now my back is old and bent
need inhalers; help pay my Rent
And you say I'm a cheat and not so dumb

Yes, I'm the bad guy, the mad guy
destroying Budget fly guy
who's never worked an honest day they say in life
who can influence their Legal Panel
when they say I'm at the flannel
but would starve without a handout in this strife.

WORKERS LAMENT TO A NON-SYMPATHETIC EAR

I thought I'd done my back in, perhaps it's mental lacking
that was never really noticed in my Claim
perceived as inefficient by reporting Inquisition
As it's deaf to any sounds involving pain

For those times when "On the Grip" I've pains from toes to hip
A bonus not foreseen by greedy mind
and on neck and lower back forever on the rack
spinal spasms plague my body all the time

My fingers ever shaking as arms and legs are aching
any medication offered rarely works
or becomes an imposition in my indigestion system
causing nasty internal bleeding they call flux

It can't be Asbestosis that charge is quite atrocious
since in Scotland it's not noted in the Courts
nor likely Emphysema as our air is so much cleaner
with no judgement for the sufferers just reports

Now regarded as a nuisance by all legal minded students
for the arguments we use to fight our Case
never coloured by any notion or co-habiting disproportion
this peculiar supposition is blamed on Celtic Race

On the Grip…Manual work paid by speed tonnage per shift usually 10 ton

THE ETHOS OF WEALTH

Do you know what bad Politicians do? Line their pockets, oh yes they do
Make up the rules with devilish tact, then abuse these rules and that's a fact
Claim huge expenses for travel and office, relatives, friends, carpets and coffees
Exempting themselves from payable tax by financial experts who know all the facts
then claim they are poor and need a pay rise while deep in manure
and surrounded in flies
Blaming the mole who's uncovered this crap by using the MET
to hunt down some chap

Do you know what bad Politicians do? Award their friends and bankers too
Give them a title and some extra cash for a sly backhander from their hidden stash
Support the bully who uses an insidious threat to extract from the voter
blood, tears and sweat
Steal from the Poor and with a grinning mask while Disabled are struggling
with an onerous task
Have several jobs but only state one. Give lowest bid contracts to brother or son.
Refuse to acknowledge their greed or their lies since elected positions
makes them elitist and wise

Do you know what bad Politicians do? Ignore all corruption while it stands
in their view
Don't raise a commotion against sleazy rules, scared of being branded
silly poor fools
Refuse to press for a change in direction while threatened by their Party
for reselection
Listen to the Whip, while ignoring the crack as the Rules in the House
move from grey to slack
Support their Leader as he demands each order, and order and order
to his million and a quarter
Yes fail to raise issue on this deep-seated infection as they ignore the day
of Election redemption.

SIREN'S SONG

At night we hear the Siren's Song, think of loved ones as time goes on
so far apart ignoring fear thoughts together feel so near

They're hunting Reporters and witnesses who have seen
the genocide of innocents to suit their leaders scheme
Rocket loaded napalm-fire extermination sweet
Conquering invaders cropping all as wheat

At night we hear the Siren's Song thoughts of loved ones as time goes on
so far apart ignoring fear thoughts together feel so near

Tonight may be our final song as shrapnel rains its tearing prong
Shooters snipe from hidden post to end each life snuff-out his ghost
Each Foreigner caught as major prize to drooling Gods with hate in eyes
Their rage so great yet never spent no depth can quench to full extent

Yet on and on the Siren's Song as War to War goes on and on
Children, innocent killed for what? The rage of man, in time forgot

DAUGHTERS OF KOBANI

As ISIS neared the city of Kobani
it was women who stood toe-to-toe
defying those monsters from Hades
when each man turned tail to go

For months they fought in that ruin
bloodied but sure in their right
Faith in their strength together
teasing those thugs with their might

Sniping from buildings of rubble
Blasting with machines made for men
Vanquished the enemy before them
from fox-hole to underground den.

Let us honour these girls for their duty
not murder or treat them with harm
See them as strength to a nation
Treat them as man would treat man

THE AGONY OF WAR

Despite the state of Country and many years of War
struggling life of Taliban we managed; but what for
One day I met the finest, finest man could be
within our love all banished, in marriage we were free

For seven years we tried, for seven years I sighed
often as we lay at night such anguish we both cried
Then one time by Allah's grace I felt within alive
patience held us both in check; we prayed it would survive

By sister's hand I was led, to hospital of care
as near to term of pregnancy, my treatment would be fair
yet at the ticking clock of time; prepared I was for section
I felt no pain at blade of knife; hope it was I mention

Relief and joy for us a boy, his name from now was Hope
And as I healed within that Ward I learn the moves to cope
I held him often to my breast; little lips to mine
Pictures flew a hundred miles to Daddy at the time

Then suddenly commotion reigned as bullets flew about
exploding shells in vivid spells death was all about
My baby died in his cot while nurses ran and screamed
blooded scores as missiles tore while battle raged and schemed

Killed twenty-six and six new babes; a feast for zealot mind
To husbands lost and lovers cost. Insane a world so blind
My mind has gone as here I lie in sister's arms sublime
O Daddy, Husband, Lover dear why us, and such a crime.

INNOCENT CHILD

She was dressed up for War today
As charcoal streaked her face
Lying there in the sewage pit
Among the soiled waste
Didn't hear the soldiers come
Her parents shot and raped
Didn't feel the slashing blade
With splitting guts a-gape

Will never learn her ABC's
Numbers one to ten
The games to play, tasks to do
With chickens in the pen
Never hear the call to prayer
Or love of girl or man
No chance of kiss goodnight
Since We don't care a damn

THEY SAID SHE SPOKE… *Improperly dressed?*

What did she do, what did she say,
she won't conform; there's no right way
they said she spoke and now the pain
within the cell each bloodied stain
and hands and feet both tied behind
to ever eat by logic mind
watered filth in sickly brew
or sleepless torment strobe-light stew
pupils locked in constant flicker
in grit-filled eyes a gaping fissure
each nail removed in silent scream
marish night in scattered dream
burned by wire each anguished rape
time stands so still it's out of date

Written during first Taliban reign

LET US REMEMBER JUNE 6 1944

Who says we're not afraid boys
                my heart is in my pants
        Can't you smell my stench of terror when ordered to advance
Did you gather up your iron nerve
                as the landing-door drops down
        To race the surf upon the sand while bullets fly around

Will we kill the enemy? A man dressed up to die
        Or have we found a resting place for my corpse to wonder why
While high above in wondrous sky stand souls in phosphorus flare
        Watchers o'er this ancient clash in dank and rank despair

For fighters who are *soldiers* ignore civilian cry
        Weeping wives who tend the fields
                as death goes rushing by
Now we stand here at attention with bugler at his post
        Salute the force of Victory,
                survivors and their ghost
But not one flag will flutter
                for each child beneath their feet
                        Innocents
        who were murdered
           to claim this day was sweet

CIVILIANS JUNE 1944

We are bombing every night now I am sure I heard the screams
of old men, kids and widows I see them in my dreams
Blood is all below me, arms and legs and feet
Scorching giants light the sky where flames and death both meet

Last night we missed our target, now all below will starve
For their fields are sown with deadly mines meant to blast Le Havre

For the soldiers on the ground now their aim is to advance
Cherbourg their objective, let civilians take their chance
Ignore their dead and dying, rape them if they cry
Like fodder to our army, their God has passed them by

And when we have won this War, no one will take the blame
For the murder of CIVILIANS as Pawns within this game!

FORGOTTEN SOLDIER

Lines never ending, onward shuffling: Civvy street welcome for the few who can cry,
we lemmings fuddling, scuffling, queuing for life, but wondering why?

Out on the road lacking the order hither and thither gone the command
patchwork the path, ruined recorder? brain in turmoil; thought in demand.

Scrambling, stumbling, grabbing, tumbling nightmares ban sleep in soporific spell
babbling, gabbling, bumbling, mumbling, Howitzer blast; what's real... can't tell!

Dodging, avoiding, bullet, mortar, sniping, blasting, killing with ease
rocket, missile, perpetuate slaughter, cannon for murder designed to please.

Crabbing the shores with desperation,scrubbing, scouring, a need to be clean
children, babies: a lost generation, blighting each moment, vivid the scene.

Escape to the land, escape from the voices; glass shards imploding again and again
trawling lost mountains, craving for choices; freedom to scream in some distant glen.

Gone is the wife; the love of the children; too late the path to therapist guide
dilemma, predicament, quandary, when? Political limbo is why he's denied!

*Remembered: an ex-soldier who lived like a hermit in fear of society on the A83 road from Glasgow
'Old Switch Back' in a clutter of scrap he called his home.*

THE RIVER OF FREEDOM

It came to me when I saw the bullet holes on the walls of houses

Freedom is a cross we have to bear
surviving wars through years of pain and tear
struggling on with knowledge we are right
fighting fear and terror through the night

Freedom is a word to give us hope
conquer chains, shackles, strangle-rope
battle through the fears that life can have
despite all prayers or gift of fatted calf

Freedom gives us strength to speak out loud
no more cowed with terror heads a-bowed
the right to write – ignore the censor talk
release the prison gates to let us walk

Freedom is the river of our soul
pushing ever onwards to its goal
seeping through all barriers in its path
washing all away within its grasp

Shout of Freedom, Stand up, stand up tall
Democracy is here for one and all
Liberty of speech in every voice
Freedom, Freedom, Freedom now rejoice.

Shout of Freedom, Stand up, stand up tall
Democracy is here for one and all
Liberty of speech in every voice
Freedom, Freedom, Freedom now rejoice.

WHEN WE WERE WEE

I remember when we were wee
you and Molly and Kenny and me
growing up the greatest of mates
never a bad word what ever the date

> Tragedy struck one day at school
> we were playing around playing the fool
> Kenny fell and a wishit it was me
> slasht awe his leg and the blood it ran free
> and it ran and it ran, but what could we do
> didn't know how, didn't have glue

Molly screamed oh she screamed he was dead
as his face went all white, the pavement was red
and, and, folks gathered round and they called for help
and Molly was cuddled for the pain that she felt

> But later that night we heard he had gone
> a far a way land where babies are born
> off to a place where children are free
> a land that was promised he'd always be

> > So now as we sit side by side on the kerb
> > or think of our pal when tucked up in bed
> > we've promised that we'll always be three
> > You and Molly and Kenny and me

POVERTY CHILD

In a room lacking hope; mice running wild
she sits all alone this poverty child
ignoring the mould, drip-drip of tap
surviving each day in a life-draining trap

Her mother has left; Crack took it's toll
Father he digs deeper into debt's hole
nothing to earn – oft threatened to pay
caught in a riddle his future is grey

Stranger in Class when going to school
hand-me-down clothes; never looks cool
invites to Sleep-overs; no chance of a friend
picked on, bullied, at games she'd attend

Would be clever at school if given the chance
few Teachers give hope or offer advance
stains mark her out when Periods start
the final straw to break a girl's heart

Will she abscond or flout every rule
follow her Mother trying to be cool
learn every trick; try to be smart
sleight with her touch or cool as a tart

Her future looks poor from teeth to toes
struggling diseases or Cancer that grows
certain to sink when deep in the mire
with Society's mind-set her future looks dire

DEATH IT'S FREE

You'll always find me here at the gate when going to School I'm never late
So be sure to get your Pills from me, yes it's true, they're really free
The ones I offer are the best no chance of side effects
Uppers, Downers what ever you want the ones I have are the ones that count
I offer more to tease the bait when you come to me – you'll need to wait

And now you're hooked you'll pay my price yes this smiling guy is not so nice
Now you say you'd like some more while you stand there at my door
You beg and plead for something stronger; a little H will zap you longer
Now you'll borrow, soon you'll steal. It's cash I need to cut a deal
Your friends are gone, family too; they've lost their bit of love for you

Soon I'll hear you're doing time; will drop your pants to score a line
Lying there in street or gutter, each day a daily flutter
That gamble once to join the crowd in dregs of life you're lying proud
Death will come to sate this lust to a starving child with a greed for Dust
Now, would you take your thrill from a guy like me,
if I promised Death and it was free?

RAPE

How can I forgive you
When you've totally destroyed my life
Each second of hell I suffered
Still feels like a twist of a knife

As a child you came to my bedroom
To touch me unlike any Dad
Tore all my organs for pleasure
Not once did you say you were bad

As a stranger you breached my defences
Attacked me for a thought of your own
Ignored any pleadings for mercy
Brutalized, naked, alone

I weep for the hours that I lay there
With tears for those years of my youth
For the love I've lost in marriage
No words can be said to soothe

I'm scarred evermore for an aeon
I'll never forgive you this crime
Despite all the Courts in this Nation
It's Me not you who does time…

KURDISH HONOUR

There is an unmarked area of our graveyard
where I visit in secret each night
My daughter refused to marry her cousin
he slaughtered her there as his right

She lies in a plot of grey silence
as many of our young girls reside
Murdered for his debt of honour
conviction to crime he's denied

A washing hangs out in public
clothing of suffrage to see
mile after mile is that clothing
reminder that skirts cannot flee

Propaganda is spread to dishonour
lies label innocents vice
shelter not offered by clansmen
sufferers treated like lice.

Be they trafficked or sold as a body,
mutilated by genital knife
suicide considered an option
avoiding murder as wife

TOO LATE TO FOSTER

The Policeman never saw as he drove on his Beat
And Social ignored me with smiles so sickly sweet
They housed me with the Perverts, men who'd leer and touch
Yet quick to chastise when I kicked one in the crutch
I know that I'm not perfect I've learn to curse and swear
But I'm struggling to survive in this place here in Tyne and Wear

They pounced on me with curry and Oriental spice
spread my body all about like dessicated rice
sucked on every morsel I was their dinner date
laughed as I lay cowering; their tasty bit of meat
semen thick and stinking from my hair to manacled feet

Found that night in river naked in the mire
called whore or cow not someone's girl lying in her byre
Was it suicide a just escape to cleanse me with the tide
that night a gang of men stole me for a ride

ADOPTION TRADE

We children are suffering at the hands of the sick
In lands round the globe we're exploited by trick
Sold in a market while ignoring our pain
A big money business where we'll never gain

We who've lost parents with no hope of care
Struggling survival often left bare
starved of affection yet sold as cheap meat
for Kidneys, Eye-balls, to medics who cheat

Held in a web of an institutionalized spider
Ghana, Cambodia, Guatemala Uganda
from Moldova, Bulgaria and the Ukraine
offered for sex in a paedophile train

Trapped in a cage yet suffering abhorrence
by Laws that deny; fuelling our sentence
Tourists may view; we're open to choice
to satisfy taste while ignoring our voice

We children are millions all round the globe
but few people speak to give us some hope
often bought to fulfil some trade
leaving us to suffer in this mental stockade.

CHEAP MEAT

I'm the product of my parents debt
coerced by threats to pay
trapped in a foreign land
my existence now looks grey

To the foreigner I'm a commodity
sold on the market of death
trapped in an alien culture
by men who would steal my last breath

You're blind when visiting a Nail-bar
cuticles more important to you
hidden the scars of suffering
when ignoring the signs of a clue

I'm there at the Car-wash
the guy who cleans and shines
not a word is spoken
all action done with signs

Gang-masters and Shell fish are tidal
picking the fruits of the sea
when beaten or drowned in waters
no trace for helpers to see

You pay by swipe or card
for the daughter you'd like to thrill
beat or rape to satisfy
for I must fit your bill

Once I hope now I'm in chains
only you can free me!

MY ENCHANTRESS OF DANCE

She sat there beside me with bright shiny eyes
points at my kilt…and asked if I'm wise…enough
to…dance for her now
She's deaf to the music it isn't surprising
been lost in a world where everyone cries in…and
suffers in pain
Her land…was the land known as Romania,
Orphaned…Imprisoned….now lives in Iberia…but
now would I dance
I danced as a man would dance for his lover
twirled on my toes like the first bulb in flower…and
worshipped her smile
She stood on her toes in a sweet pirouette
a moment of grace…her neat silhouette…as
she danced for me then
I saw in her years complete dedication
a gift that she had her skill of expression…in
a ten year old child
She showed in her dance the pain of her suffering
the fight to survive to me so unnerving…oh
how she could dance
And now that I've gone…I'll treasure the moment
though my tears may be old…my heart ran the gamut…of
wonder in smiles
I wander the streets I've lost all direction
locked in my head…each step of perfection…to
My Enchantress of Dance
and I'll never forget the time…and the moment…of
I'll never forget the time…and the moment of…then

IN PERFECT UNION

I met my Love at a ceilidh in the village hall one night
Our eyes just met as though by fate upon the tinder-light
Within his hand my little hand was soon held tight in clasp
And promised both to be by troth at end of summer's mark

From Raerinish Point, on Wedding Day, my Love and kin set sail
I would not trust the weeping wind, for my Love could never fail
Come dawn the news; the tragedy; the numbness and the pain
I lost all hope of will to live, no one could I blame

I would not eat, refused to drink, in hope that I might die
To lie beside my Love in Death, to give me peace to cry
Within three weeks I'd passed away, lying in my room
To Rodel grave I would be put, within my family tomb

As the ship sailed o'er the sea, its crew were wracked with doubt
Would cast my coffin overboard; were quick to put about
The tides and currents chopped and changed, then carried me ashore
Upon an Isle of Shiant lay, my coffin battered, sore

And as this worthless shell it broke, but left my body hale
I lay within my Lover's arms and kissed his pallid veil
A Lewis man from Gravir Town found us lying there
As tears were running down his cheeks, he would not see us bare

He left us there in full caress upon the lapping shore
And bade them all to leave us there, not visit any more
To leave me in my Lover's arms, by Chance or Love or Fate
By weeping wind and fetching sea upon our Wedding Date

A FRIEND

I can remember that day we walked up the hill
with the chill creeping in and the air so still
when the children were racing to play in the snow
happy screams of delight, each face all a-glow.
We talked of the struggle through each day of pain
you fighting cancer each op. such a drain.
Me with my problem where none could agree
about Parkinson's, M.S. or maybe M.E.
Your chance of survival. My hope of cure
our wars of depression, life insecure
Family, friends their support and concern
despite arguments, tempers they didn't earn
and the chance of a future despite each relapse
with a minute of stoic perhaps, just perhaps.

The pleasure you had at the birth of your daughter
each day in your arms, the words that you taught her
going to school I saw hope in your eyes
each day of her life held a special surprise.
For me I had gained a fantastic new clan
granddaughters, grandsons, now part of their plan
and at times when I felt I couldn't go on
I would think of their feelings if I was gone.

I left you then and climbed up the hill
for each step that I took left a deep thrill
while I looked all around at the children at play
Was coaxed on a sledge; it lit up my day
Now my life has returned I was given the answer
While you bravely fought on...now gone...to...

MINER'S WIFE'S LAMENT

Yi saed yi loved mi whin wi met
Yi loved mi whin wi married
Sae hurry hame wi yir wage poke
My love yi need-nae tarry

Wiv naethin in thi hoose tae eat
Thae cupboards urr awe empty
Sae hurry hame wi yir wage poke
An weel hae broth a-plenty

Oor Bairnies jeel in thaer wee bed
Thi cauld iz wapt aroon thim
Sae hurry hame wi yir wage poke
An thaell hae heat atween thim

A ken yi need tae drink wae boe-ys
Yir joe-b iz dark an scary
Bit bring uz hame yir wage poke
An weel bi thaer tae cheer yi

A hope yi huv nae drunk thi nicht
A pray thit yi urr sober
Tae bring uz hame yir wage poke
Am feart yill beat mi o'er

Aye yince a met thi finest man
A miner an a lover
Bit noo A'v lost him tae thi drink
A darnae peat hiz brither

LOST THI WIFE

It's twa years since a loast thi wife
Hur goin wiz hard, no it jist wisnae nice
An folks huv been grand, thae couldnae a-done mair
Tae ease thae days whi a felt sae sair

The Socials bin roon an thiv sent a young lass
Shi diz awe ma clase tae hur its nae fash
It's whin she gans hame, that a feel it thi maist
A mind fur a meenit shi wiz thair az ma guest
Richt at that oor whin shi gans oot thi yett
A remembir thi wife an thi day thit wi met

A'm share shi caws frae the tap o thi stair
An A'll gan an look, bit thir's naebudy there
A'll try tae read an licht a smoke
Pace the carpet bit its awe a joke
At nicht a jist canna settle
Ma heid a'll bi birlin its no in fine fettle

Hud a word wae thi Doectar aboot me naw sleepin'
Hi offirt Pills bit that's jist cheatin'
An shi didnae believe aboot thae knock-oot things
urr the effect o drink an whit it brings
Awe whit can a dae tae git oor thi loss
wae ma lassie gan
an shi's left mi thi Boss!

AT DAWN

I've lost the way to climb today each step I meant to take
Leads me past the hills I knew and paths my boots would make
I've seen the deer in battling form in herds a thousand strong
The blackcock dance in strut and tut afore the sun at dawn

I've see the hills a-running with burns so thick with foam
The heather soaked and glistening and bog-oak bleached like bone
I've heard the screaming plover cry with whirling beats so strong
As curlew mourn the dotterel pipe on tundra moors at dawn

I've see the hares a-skipping in brown to brilliant white
And corries deep in winter snow from blue to purple bright
Icicles flash a twinkling each droplet bathed and drawn
And moonbeams march in shadowed form afore the light of dawn

I've seen the steps of innocence striding in the snow
Of birds unknown and little beasts and animals as they go
And lava flows and pebbles dash with mica rapt and torn
For all my years as I did walk upon the hills at dawn

Now I've lost the way to climb today for each step that I took
My map in head has lost all sight I dare not stand and look
By compass line and north degree baptised but not been born
For now I've lost that final year to walk the hills at dawn

PROMISE

If I should succumb to an illness
don't let me waste away
Don't let them feed me potions
forever and a day
Think of me as a your lover
and what I'd really want
Not sitting here a lonely death,
grey and pale and gaunt
Will you take me to the hill dear
to a place that I might lie
Then leave me though it hurts dear,
for me to stay and die
I know for you it would be painful
to leave me in this way
For you know that I would die my love
before the end of day
So take me to the mountains
and sit me in the snow
Say you love me one last time,
you know my pain won't show
One day upon the hill
is nought compared to years
To tending me an empty man
through aching soulful tears.

THOSE MORNING BLUES

As I strolled out one early morn
by the light it was well past dawn
as the dew on the grass twinkled and shone
that pink on the clouds had almost gone
the leaves were rustling in a zephyr like breeze
I could hear the birds twitter up in the trees

With this thought in my head it turned to food
in the mood I was in it could do me some good
then I espied a young girl in a long black coat
with bright yellow boots, it put a lump in my throat
she was walking along with her head in the sky
that girl was a beauty I felt I must try

But as I approached she skipped to one side
as the sight of those thighs left me fit to be tied
then I drew nearer she took wings and flew
when you're stalked by a cat it's the right thing to do!

ABSOLUTELY

There's a word going round, we hear it every day
It's Absolutely!
Yes used in every context and any type of way
It's Absolutely!

We hear it on the radio and now it's on the Net
Once it was a certainty with every type of bet
In every conversation or there's someone you've just met
But Absolutely

I'm sure it came from London where living is so fast
Where people speak English in a high or lower caste
And millionaires make billions that leave us all aghast
Oh Absolutely

You'd never hear Biden say it, Donald would object
While Republicans would argue with the wording so select
As Putin would try to use it like a virus to infect
It's Absolutely

You'd never hear Rees Mogg say it as he thinks he's upper crust
Or Truss, Patel or Bannerman as they grind us into dust
Or that Labour Leader? who thinks his claim is just
Yes Absolutely

The Chancellor is saying his purse-strings must be tight
And our PM is certain that their policies are Right
While the majority are suffering with nothing left to bite
It's Absolutely

It's Absolutely, not Certainly, or Totally, or Wholly
Nothing but Absolutely will do
Truly Absolutely

THE CAT AND THE FIDDLE

What's this I spy with my little eye the lounge door is lying wide open
with some luck – and a whim I will tip toe in they'll be no one there I'm hoping
I'll get up on the couch and there I will crouch then snuggle deep into a cushion
I'll hide in its pile just for a while I'm sure I'll not be a nuisance

Well after a while, whilst in my pile I heard the most terrible screeching
ooo what pain to a friend on a scale … about ten and its effect on me
was terribly outreaching
I shot from the spot as if I'd been shot and tried to escape by the door
what could I say to get me away as this noise scared me right to my core

Out in the hall I banged into the wall then skidded right into the kitchen
oh I was sore as I pleaded not more my friend is suffering from friction
well the noise it soon stopped then I paused—then I hopped
I was worried my poor friend had died
I crept into the room by what or by whom it was then that I sat down and cried

He just lay on a chair quite fur-less and bare and his neck was stretched for a yard
his ears they looked queer set-off in a tier whatever had happened was bad
So I sat on the mat a..a sad little cat watched my friend being stuffed in his place
not a squeak did he cry as I heard the lid sigh of a Fiddle being put in its case

THE PIPER'S CAVE

Above our town the Piper's cave few dare enter, none but brave
Many tales of Witch and spells piping drones with chiming bells
held us kids in dread and fear of corpses ghouls on floating bier
Some mining men took the task with lamp in hand and dram in flask
to search the truth or likely tale feel the fear; would they fail?

Squeezing through the tightest gaps avoiding waters nasty traps
climbing over rocks and boulder sweating, struggles, strata colder
At slimy fissure split in two which to take there was no clue
Carefully they tied a cord then to a chance on right-hand fork
Ahead there appeared a solid wall all reverse the urgent call

Tripping o'er rocks stones soon was heard the moans of groans
At left-hand fork Tam took the lead on glancing down saw a reed
from out a chanter from the past, picked it up and gave a blast
Hairs were quickly stood on end glad no ghoul but Tam their friend
then saw the bones of ancient Piper with fear in heart, action hyper

Men took leg with cautious speed to climb back out they all agreed
Say no more with nowt to say leave the Cave for another day

THE US FARMER'S COVID LAMENT

This f…n' virus it's killin' ruinin' all our trade
No more Fast Food industry everythin' now home made
they're re-learnin' home bakin' bread and cookies too
I can see us all goin' Bankrupt God, tell me what to do

No one wants our Chicken Wings or Beef is now mis-steak
our Porkers all are squealin' their feeding gone to cake
Donald said we all must eat but this virus here is loose
No one wants to work now to sue is their excuse

All our Cream for Coffee is goin' down the drain
with Cows all a-moanin' their udders such a pain
We've now a Butter mountain Cheese you just can't freeze
and our Hens ignore the message with Eggs up to our knees

With Pizzas goin' to pieces all the boys laid off
and no one wants delivery from a guy whose got a cough
No one keen on Curries for chance they get the bug
Hot-dogs off the menu it's time to pull the plug.

No ones pickn' Grapes now or harvestin' the crop
O God please tell me when will this all stop!!

A BLOODY MIX UP

We're having to set a precedent Sir
On which blood would you like
Since all the bloods now mixed here
We can't offer Black or White

Now we've searched the World over
And come up with Packs to use
If you fill in our Questionnaire
I'm sure we'll do for you

Ah! You are Jew Sir
and German not too pure
European is quite dodgy
We can't promise any cure

Black is recommended Sir
But..we could weaken it with Bleach
Or we've a batch of Native American
Due here within the week

Of course you can have Red Sir
But..is it really what you want?
Moscow will be delighted
With China keen to taunt

May we go for Regular?
The safest we would say
You've a good chance it'll be fine Sir
It's only sourced from Gay

Trump's Father as a German claimed he was a Jew to prevent Incarceration during the War
He often changed his past Nationality to suit the situation

YIN SMERT POACHER

Ootside thur hoose, thi storm wid rage, hur man wiz share a trust'd sage
Hi kent thi nicht whur keepir be, tae fish fur troot at pool oan Dee
In poke hi pit sum breed an' line, hiz tin o hooks furr fish tae dine
Carrot net tae hod thi catch, kiss tae wife an lift't latch
Frae lammin' shed hi taen hiz coat, check'd each pooch furrr owt furgoat
thin strode wae pace tae face thi nicht, bood tae gale weel tack't tae ficht

Till doon aside thae waatirs black, oily, burlin, edd'd slack
Taen hiz tackle frae hiz pooch, set his lines furr fish tae mooch
Swung thim roon an cast awe oot, thin bid hiz peace oan sodden root
Sax times cast thin yin mair, tae tease thi cratir frae it's lair
Frae line in han hi sneck'd tae stane if owt a-boot hi feart thur gain
Slipp'd aff laik hoolet ghoul nae chance wae owt o ghillie's fool

Wae-in sum trees hi'd bide hiz time, strain hiz lugs furr soond urr sign
Thin whin share frae lug an' ee, slips sleekit like frae a-hint thi tree
Un-hanks thi line slips net in pool draws in hiz catch wae movement cool
Hiz lug it twtch't wae wheesh't in whin, hi slipp't hiz coat frae ither skin
Ease'd awa frae castin' spot thae men wurr oot an hi wiz hot
Yet naen gan chase, awe wiz peace, furr aw thae fund an auld ewe fleece!

THE GHOST O FISHIN' PAST

Frae Port Seton, Cockenzie an Fisherraw, we sailed aboot the sea
Chasin' Silver Darlin's whur ever thae may be
North tae Shetland waters Sooth tae Grimsby toon
Wae Luggers, Zulus, Drifters thur dearth cam ower soon

Bi inshore it wiz handline in deep wi shot lang Seine net
Corralled them tae pull them in wae burnin' hands an' sweat
In awe the ports aboot oor land wur lassies guttin' fish
Sautin' them in barrels gae-in pickin's fur the rich

Noo on the West Coast bi Tarbert thae argid thae wur right
Tae trawl thae fish wae a singal boat an thae wur keen tae fight
It wiz argid in the House ae Lords fur few wur keen tae back them
thae fisherfolk wur treated bad noo awe aboot wid thank them

As time went by the Ruskies came an yins frae the Common Market
Fishin' wae the finest mesh it wiz an awfie basket
Oor North Sea's laik a desert noo wae argid wae commotion
An noo wur telt tae throw them back bi scientific notion

Crab an' Lobster noo the catch fur linin' foreign dishes
Since boats gan oot wi toorists noo wae oor sea sae scarce o fishes

ON DISTANT SHORE

He sailed the seas in a house of steel
Near and far with ports unreal
Sunsets gloried grey to red
Pressured glass, could drop like lead

Been becalmed in torpid sea
Thick kelp fields with plastic free
Battled waves that turned men sick
Roiled in breakers mountains thick

North and South through cracking ice
Mortal combat freed by dice
Trolled the ocean East or West
Health oft strained by Disease or pest

In ports he sampled Orient fare
Spice streets of bodies bare
Curried colour in every hue
Drunken days; non-stop spew

Days now passed with memories old
He feel the aches when muscles cold
Reflecting moments ebb and flo
Of days gone past on distant shore.

IN ANCIENT SPORT

We dapple waters clear and bright
Across great pools of mirrored light
Escaping glints cascading sight
In shadows deep as black as night
Cast by cast in whip-like motion
On rippled glass of spilling lotion
Snaking out through teasing potion
A tempting prize from out the ocean

Trout and salmon, mighty prey
Hear our prayer to you this day
Seek to hunt our dappled fly
For every cast by line we ply
Then run and dance and ply and fight
Tax our skill to wrest your might
Trick and skive, be-still the water
Yes teach us well you great globetrotter

From every land you hear our boast
In rushing spate or delta coast
By desert sands we burn or roast
With finest cane to bear the force
Angler, fisher, net or line
In bated breath await your sign
As each at post await forlorn
So sure you'll come, as sun at dawn

A COXSWAIN'S TRIAL

You stand every day at the Quay-side
with a ghost at the end of your sleeve
Locked in your memory that terrible day
It's hard for a Coxswain to grieve
In the Graveyard is a stone to their memory
each name etched deep in mind
When the maroons went off a warning
To the storm that was one of a kind

Force twelve and the glass it was dropping
To a freighter breaking up on a reef
to a man they came on his order
Trust in their Coxswain, their Chief
They say men never cry with emotion
when you've lost everyone of your crew
The boat overturned in the maelstrom
What can man in heart do

Let us all weep for them lost in the Ocean
Let us all weep for those lost in the sea
O God as this Coxswain before you
How can I ever be free?

ON THE FACE OF BEN NEVIS

Lochaber M.R.T.

I remember it well, in those long fifty years when us boys on a Shout
lost many tears
a Honeymoon couple descending the Ben, Five degrees out meant nothing to them
They slid down the slope losing control bounced and rolled faster into a bowl
stopped by an ice-axe yet battered and bruised struggled to crawl,
then secured with ice-screws

Late for their date; the Police were alerted; A rescue was likely they quickly asserted
but where on the Ben? It was a bit of a worry the obvious place
was Five-Finger Gully
On the hope we were right we raced for the mountain scrambling the gully
with prayer in our heart
snow falling heavy we fought on the ledges into the basin
where the couple were trapped

A stretcher was needed when we studied his leg. She in deep shock from the cut
on her head
We splinted and bandaged then offered food, paired each in sleeping bags
as best as we could
Winds screamed with rage as snow fell harder, cutting our breath
like a Heilan-man's garter,
He moaned for his wife's fight the night's cancer. She died in my arms
as she offered no answer

It is hard to think what was the right way something I explore day after day
Fifty years gone I've thought through their descent. Our route of approach;
hurried hell-bent
Should we have done this, or that? Her loss to me still a pain to my heart

Five-Finger Gully is a dangerous place the slightest error is all that it takes
a step from the path to lose control on snow and ice in a murderous bowl
Few have survived this thousand foot brawl, those that have face a sheer waterfall
not fit to climb up to a refuge terrace without any help, those fallen will perish.

QUAKE

Feb. 22 2011 NZ

I see   each page
                of my jotter
                    flicker down   through
motes   of grey dust
          Wails...scream in my ear
as rocks slither   and scrape around
Fear...Oh Fear   to hear   distant ...drip of cold
                      blood?
      all is dark   dust slips ...
in trickles ...hunting new path   on my face
A shiver ... which way up ...or?   One second of ...crack
      we? lie trapped ...locked in a virgin world
    Trapped !
Sweat   oozes hot .. cold...shiver
       screams !!.pain ?..or fear
sobs murmur
       Light daggers in through sliding steps grey, cream sticky
mud ...or blood
              drip...erratic...drip
  invading silence   high high above
I hear them
          ant-like...scratching, scraping
               thirst invades
slabs slide ....of WHAT!...Fear...a scream from me within?
      Donk – Donk – Donk
Whine on Steel...Sparks dance around my tomb
          stink of burning.....metal?
      What ever happened to...each page has gone
    as ...one by one
...my tears dry ......within
     this crust of Death....

A SINGLE USE MASK

A single use mask is where all our sins hide
We're featureless beings with Virus denied
Where some people dump as never before
all types of trash and masks on the floor

So relieved at Survival with attitude blasé
they ignore everybody. See things their way
No more the Highwayman or stranger in dress
with lack of expression to hide our distress

Endless the tide
Endless the waves
Endless the plastic
When nobody cares

Our lives are threatened drowning within
as ignorance pervades those with thick skin
For they are the problem with Libertine views
Manipulating science while hiding the clues

DARE YOU DRINK IT?

But do you know what some farmers do?
Scatter on their fields Human Poo
SEPA permitting in all their tests
ignoring the fact that it's us who ingest
blind to chemicals and new fangled metals
Drugs legal and some accidental

Mixtures that react while high in the air
With substances from industry floating spare
In this Scientific age few people care
what is served in a restaurant as ideal fare!

When you drink bottled water is it really pure,
no added ingredients of industrial manure?
Thoroughly filtered by a Highland spring
or historical bacteria time can bring
But are there checks for modern infections?
where knowledge is needed for accurate detection
When opening a bottle will you stop and think
Are you really certain it is safe to drink?

SOMETHING TO BEEF ABOUT

They are clearing the Amazon forest to ensure you've cheap meat on your plate
Killing off indigenous peoples to be sure you've always a steak
Careless of their Carbon Footprint no matter how high are the waves
When greedy for meat on the table – as Meat is something folk craves

How many will argue with Lidl – discounters searching a price
Sainsbury, Tesco or Walmart, their profiting ain't very nice
Aldi, Morrison or Co-op promoting organic and green
Coming from the Amazon jungle – who knows the process it's seen

There's some dubious folk in the Market, Marfrig and Vestey are two
Controlling most of the shipping – Beef is what they both do
Feeding our boys in the Army to an MOD desperate to waste
Contracts are given to cheapest, lost is the corruption and taste

Greed is a necessary evil when clearing a forest or two
Killing of creatures and natives is required when taking this view
Yet we are the ones on this diet not starving for want of a meal
Closing our eyes to this madness of the Salesmen who offer a deal

School meats sourced out of the country – Hospitals packaged so neat
Austerity is Government practice; this price can never be beat
Ignored is the label Buy British, when there's not enough to go round
As our farmers rely on a hand-out – or their business will go under the ground

Let's stop this waste of our jungles
Syphon off some of the wealth
End the destruction for cattle
Think of this Earth and its health.

KING CARBON

This world is in the grip of a Pandemic
a disease that's attacking each mind
this is the worst type of infection
for it can affect all of Mankind

It can't be cured with a vaccine
It needs a change in the way we all think
for we're destroying the World with our actions
yet few will notice the stink
We're choking the oceans with plastic
Waste is dumped in the sea
Chemicals mixed form potions
over lands where it shouldn't be

We're brainwashed with King Carbon
Plastic is not what it seems
Obviously not good for our Planet
yet ignorance is driving our dream
Yes every Government is tidal
Motions stuck on the ebb
While storms are raging on shorelines
Those drowning are stuck in a web

THE GREENHOUSES OF ALMERIA

How is Spain accepted in Europe
when Slavery is close to its heart
Folks from the African continent
Suffer from the first day they start
Working under Plastic
Living to harvest a crop
50 degrees no shade for some
When will this madness stop

Billionaires are living off Plastic
Feeding us all on the cheap
Careless of workers or Environment
we shoppers are all fast asleep
No one thinks of the Tomato or Melon
Lettuce produced by the tonne
Packaged by African children
in a factory where work's never done

Hectares and metres of Plastic
dumped when finished in use
All around the Med fish are dying
It's cheap they say as excuse
The same for the African people,
enslavement is cheap at a price
Yet no argument is raised in Brussels
Perhaps they've been offered a slice

DO I SMELL A RAT

Because of some B's
More than one or two
this nation we love
is becoming a loo
Baby-wipes, nappies and plastic
Crap from the lazy
in our Country
Tragic!
Black bags of Litter
mixed in with Cat
While moaners complain
at seeing a Rat
Yet blind to Gulls
Magpie and Crow
as carry-out wrappers
steadily grow

Behaving like pigs
Am I beginning to bore?
These two-legged creatures
come to the fore
Dumping their trash
in sight of a Bin
ignorant slobs
drop it and grin

This is an Offence
but cheap is the fine
if caught in the act
They should do time!

AN IMMEDIATE EFFECT

It is well past time when we gave a thought to protecting our environment;
not a little – a lot
As long as profit reigns supreme saving this Planet has remained a dream

Now Mother Nature, she needs a hand
for dealing with Mankind, his growing demand
to exterminate creatures because they are there with a greed for themselves;
no need to care
Choke us with litter, be it plastic or paper, Dioxins, Chemicals
and toxic vapour
Hearing damage from continuous noise while blinding with Science
and useless toys

      You don't think so?

Did you check out the Toothpaste you put on your teeth?
and the fine print wording seen underneath
Triclosan was used until not long ago,
environmentally toxic; did anyone know?

Who checked out the Teflon on pan or wok
about deadly Cancers; or perhaps not
Who studies chemicals for cause and effect?
Since Lawyers win, few items are checked

Those wonderful veggies we get from afar
in what are they washed? Some chemical tar?
We hear of the Yanks' chicken and meat.
Do other countries set out to cheat?

Folks drink water in bottles of plastic
Does plastic poison? Now that would be tragic!

RUNNING MAN

I'm running from the North   I'm running from the South

   I'm never ending running pulling plastic from my mouth

I'm running from the Climate
            I'm running from the wind

                        I'm running from the greed of man

      with Treaties he has signed

I'm running from the melting ice   my land a raging fire

      I'm running from the future Wars
                        what I see is dire

I'm running from the rising seas my land to disappear

   I'm running in this endless race it's end of hope I fear

CULL OF THE WILD

Who cries for the earth
when the ground is torn
to make way for the site
of a house to be born
As turf is rolled up
with its carpet of history
Battles, deaths
Blessings or misery

Mourning the loss of
sound in this park
Insects, Corncrakes
Crickets and Larks
Meadow flower vivid
whish blown grass
lost to the future
Yesterday past

FUTURE CHILD – TOMORROW BELONGS TO ME

The sun on the meadow is scorching the grass – there's no escape in the sea
As the waters rise drowning the land our leaders refuse to agree
Solar collectors and windmill blades stir up disagreements of freeze
while coal and oil help arguments boil and nuclear lasts for years

Promotions of poisons while no one cares – killing the moth and the bee
While children are singing in our streets – Tomorrow belongs to me
Jungles removed for meat on the hoof, as temperatures rise in the sea
Ice lands are melting for the greed of man, while Powers refuse to agree

The creation of plastic has turned to tragic with acres polluting the sea
while litter and glitter blight the land, no one is pointing at me
Folks fly round the world in ignorance bold yet campaign to be carbon free
ignoring the damage done on earth as pollutants fall down to the sea

The babe in the cradle is closing its eyes – the blossom embraces the bee
But now says a whisper from future child – Tomorrow belongs to me
Palm trees are showing where forests were growing and animals roamed to be free
Now creatures are dying despite children trying as industry kills by degree

With the words Trump is saying our Planet is paying each treaty is dumped
with a tweet
while Americans are frying, drowning and dying and poor are thick on the street
The babe in the cradle is closing its eyes – the blossom embraces the bee
But all will be lost if they don't take care – as tomorrow belongs,
Yes tomorrow belongs, tomorrow belongs to me!

A COVID MOMENT STOLE

As I walk along the Learside nearby Glen Ramskill burn
Watching eel and dogfish do their twist and turn
Then stravaig recent bulldozed track unsteady on my pins
Onwards ever upwards past fresh the scent of whins

Oh to be in heather upon the mountain ling
skarting boots and gaiters, scented flowers sing
Passing o'er the Piper's Cave perchance a skirl or moan
Steady onwards to the Goat memories flood: I'm home

Tears of joy ignore the call 'Go Back' by welcome Grouse
Youth upon Beinn Ghuilean escape from pain and house
Below the farm at Crosshill a moment lost in thought
Days of skinny dipping our path now just a blot

Times spent in the Valley, nuts for all to eat
Spooning out the ground-nuts and soorucks we thought sweet
The Goat has slid into History by Foresters lacking care
and the path we walked the Damhead jungled track nightmare

Shooting hares at Tomaig; pheasants on the run
Picnics at the Black Loch, singing larks in sun
Bypass the tree invasion this day I'll need to thole
going down the Kileonan ridge a Covid moment stole.

GREAT AUNT

Rag rugs we'd see in a-plenty, great dust motes hung in the air
A box-bed curtained from viewers while caged birds whistled their air
Spiders played catch in the windows tatted fine lace in each trap
Blue-bottles buzzed in a death-knell as sunbeams fought through the gaps

Newspapers littered the table, an argument raged on each print
Underlined words in each sentence highlighted with Indian ink
An organ sat dumb in a corner peddled from some distant shore
Harbouring memories of family; riddled with woodworm and more

Her garden a jungle of promise from cuttings of something she'd seen
Tropicals lush and enticing to Emperors, Monarchs or Queen
Hens clucked about in a corner searching for eggs that they laid
As a goose gave honk in excitement could be a gold one she'd made?

Our visits were rare, on occasion she tended to scare away folks
By cursing she did on a Sunday at all those dressed in fur coats
Of the men with white gloves and Trilby, "A Bunnet wiz fine" she would say
"Thi pair hae nowt tae bi sertin wull thi Lord no visit that day."

Never saw a doctor or a Church Minister in her adult years. She died aged 94 outliving four local doctors!

DIDN'T SEE MAGPIES

When I was a boy I didn't see Magpie but Corncrakes, Peewits often in field
Curlews or Whaps mournful at sunset Partridge and Pigeon grubbing a meal
Unknown to me the Lark in accension; rarely saw Oysters except on Ice-cream
Never saw Sable or Coney except on fur coats; a night at the Pictures
we stood for the Queen

Rarely saw Basking Sharks but Herring saw plenty;
never saw Whales splash in our seas
Read in the Eagle of Dan Dare and Spaceships;
pleasures with friends one terrible freeze
Never saw pens except with an inkwell, pencils and chalk we used when at school
Suffer in Barbers when they used Clippers, mechanical things to make us look cool

Never saw Jet Planes to fly high above us; Steam Road-Rollers clanked in our Street
Nuclear Plants with giant Water-Coolers, a dream for the Future's Mechanical feat
Often I watched the man from the Gas-works draining the stink from the sump
in the street
Coal lit the fires to heat us in winter few dried the Moss others called Peat

Never saw Pepsi or sweet orange Fanta, Ginger was flavours in bottles neat
Deposit we got returns for our pocket, cans of aluminium soon had them beat
Hedges were cut by hard sweating Hedge-men teams in a line steady and slick
Occasional pause to stroke of a Whetstone constant level to height of the stick

Harvest gateways cleared for horses, Scythe mowing grass in silent swirl
Balers stood clanking belted to tractor, Hay knitted package binded by purl
Motor cars started by using a handle; Flick of the wrist – sudden back-fire
Foxes roam the streets as we wonder Cheetahs in Government will they retire?

GAIRLOCH VIEW

I see the past before me in ancient silhouette
Its ridges, peaks and gorges ingrained with none to vet

That dance upon a wet Dun Can; lost tears to Clachan cleared
Eagles soar o'er Brittle Glen those memories deeply seared

By Elgol grave on high cliff path as waters fight below
Then ripping razors tear at legs when battling rage of bore

A hammered blow on slate-less roof as Bothy broke the gale
While finger-food squelched at our feet with tea in can to bail

With fear in heart the route they'd part
avoid 'Bad Step' they plead
Up and over each one cries
Yet I must take the lead

Then eagle flash by stumbling dash
Its barn-door raised before us
While maelstrom sky
unleashed lead dye
Each lochan dimpled, porous

An Dorus a Cuillin spot
beguiled by Great Stone Chute
Ten step back to one step on
by bouldered dust and boot

A CLASS IN MILLKNOWE

Where are they now the Class of Miss Ellis
Archie and Angus and both Christine's too
Alistair and Jim and Elsbeth and Diane
Where are they now and what do they do

Where has Jane gone or David or Ian
Gordon or Willy or Mary and Ann
Jean and wee Jean, Janet and Robert
Memories of then by this an old man

And Toby and Alison, Kenneth or John
Katrina or Elizabeth, who sat in that Class
Survivors or Pensioners, residing or travelled
One moment's reflection in fragments of glass

IN HARVEST PAST

Rise to work by first dawn ray, breakfast fed for harvest day
pocket whetstone, piece and cap
fill tin flask from running tap and pat for pipe once more

Shoulder scythe from hook on rack, hessian sheet off cut wool sack
step by stride and rolling gait
the moment's come its ne'er to late to check for pipe once more

To clear the gate for Fordson tractor, cutter, baler then extractor,
piece by piece in hessian sheet
each sheaf of gold so meadow sweet as arcs the scythe once more

Swathe by slice of fan-like grass swirled on ground by scythe blade pass
then turned and spread for sun to bake
by sweated palm and guided rake scrape wooden pegs once more

Day on day each stalk is turned dried so dry but never burned,
fearful eye on cloudy weather
steady pace in constant measure as children play once more

Onto stook then raised to rick by twist of wrist on pitchfork flick
sheaf by sheaf to dry for bale
packed tight dry all sweet and hale its time has come once more

Begone this gold by lassies keen on loaded carts in lustre sheen
to store in barn or dry hay shed
for winter's feed and cattle fed with harvest done once more

DEPRESSION VIEW

A climb upon the Buachaille
Reflected sit
with char on Tower

Alone in peace

Tranquillity
That moment stole an hour
beyond
expanse of Rannoch
yet turmoil
still within

Years of tears and struggle

till joy
the scent of Whin.
if there be a God
be it a mountain
or
the sea
To us lost within this desert of –

Depression

it takes one moment to be
free

ON REFLECTION

I'm starving for the moment and eating for your love
I hate to see this figure, there's nothing left to rub
Some say I'm anorexic, others say I'm sick
But I need the perfect figure how I do it is the trick

Yet I'm gorging for the moment then I'll spew the whole lot up
then blame myself for bingeing; bingeing not enough
then I'll cry in desperation; depression is for slobs
that my body is revolting and I'm looking at a blob

Now I know that I'm bulimic it is what the doctor said
had all the pills to prove it, this notion in my head
but what they call a remedy I know it isn't true
O mirror what I really need is trust and love from you

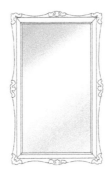

JAMES

A jist sit here worryin', worryin' awe thi time
A cannae sleep wi worryin' A'll soon go oot ma mine

Jist yin chance tae hae ma ain hoose, whin A've nivvir biled a kettle
gain a chance tae smoke a fag, az thi winae let mi settle

A wa-anted tae live here jist live here ba-masell
Hoo wis A tae ken I'd bi lonely A really couldnae tell

A jist feel sae lonely sittin ba-masell
nae budy tae tak tae it maks me sic unwell

Demands cum in broon envelopes awe thi wa-ant is money
Demandin' demandin' awe thi time it really isnae funny

Letters frae the Cooncil threats tae kick mi oot
Demands, demands fir hunners thi dinnae care a hoot

A jist sit here worryin' smokin' awe thi time
A cannae sleep wi worryin' A'll soon go oot ma mine

MY MUM – YOUR MUM

She sits alone in an empty box
Hair bedraggled tangled locks
Language confused limited sentence
Repeated phrase lacking essence
Angry at loss, violent, baffled
Morose, tearful, mumbling, garbled

Beside her sits a cup or glass
Why is it there? A moment. Pass
Incontinence common, urine infection
Few clues to the sufferer chancing detection

Isolated from all; surrounded by company
Animated chattering never in harmony
Bewildered subject monotonous theme
Lost in fracture yesteryear dream

Dementia – the terrible Disease

PATIENT DEATH

What's the point of sitting here
sitting all alone
when I'm sitting here suffering
each breath to keep me going
It's pills that keep me living,
inhalers let me breathe
I'm dying of emphysema
I just crackle and I wheeze

What's the point of living
suffering this existence
What's the point of all these pills
I'll never go the distance
O please God take me in my sleep
or another day will pass me by
another day I'll weep

ARTERIAL PREDICAMENT

Do you know what some lazy folk do
sit on their laurels, oh yes they do
Not the likes of me and you
We need to exercise, yes all of us do

They sit every day for hours on their bum
letting their arteries thicken with gum
Ignoring the risk of death by a stroke
Treating all warnings as simply a joke

Poo-pooing their chances of an untimely risk
of damage to joints or a vertebral disc
infections to chest or maybe Diabetes
while stuffing their faces with sugary sweeties

Drinking pure glucose in a cheap fizzy drink
while testing the levels their bodies will sink
as they guzzle up rubbish not fit for the tip
becoming more bloated and ready to rip

Ignoring good fibre, lean meat or rice dish
Forgetting the benefit of oil in cod fish
Refusing to eat apples, bananas or pears
Fresh green vegetables; nobody cares

No need for a walk or run up some stairs,
cycle to work; rather slouch in a chair
Never climb hills to take in the view
Yes! Telly's the thing when you don't have a clue!

WARNING! WARNING! WARNING!

Sugar And Spice are not all things nice,
their excess can lead to **Diabetes**
They will suck you in
to their greatest sin
presented to you as good sweeties
Whether tempted by wrapping
or thick chocolate coating
a devil is hiding inside
Blindness or worse
can become a huge curse
or Death can knock at your door
Think this a moan
going on an on
but the treatment's
persistent and sore
Please heed this advice
yes it's not very nice
A Warning you cannot ignore!!

LIBERTY, EQUALITY, FRATERNITY

You have killed our tree of Life with your Nuclear knife
on the day of Two Suns in the Sky
No more will it seed or flower it is dying by the hour
Deaf to our suffering and our cry

Your Caucasian might snuffed out our candle of night
Cursed the Pacific nations with a blast
Blighted the seas around and all deep within the ground
Stained our existence for our future now is cast

Now we die each day from Cancers; you never give answers
to Jellied creatures to our women each day born
Kids are ill misshapen often wounds lie a-gaping
leaving us to cope with what to us is foreign.

No offer of assistance from your parliament of distance
Genocide of life a distant clue
for never would we know till we felt its mighty blow
what was sacrificed on that moment just for you.

You steal and kill for greed which you justify as need
Indigenous a blight on profits it is said
Your Christian God is white believing you are right
and the only good native there is dead.

You refuse to see our view of oceans that once were blue
Choked the fishes and creatures of the seas
exterminate animal and bird when they won't do as bid
killed our Islands of any future in these years

Due to Atomic & Nuclear testing the Indigenous Peoples continue to suffer!

CHRISTIAN CONTRACT

Once it was written in the Bible Commandments set out in stone
For those who were baptised Christian to all people this religion be known
Each agreed to the terms of the Contract to treat everyone with respect
But where does it say in the Bible which peoples you're allowed to reject

Is there a Chapter that identifies others The Black, the Yellow, the Red
Natives from jungles or islands for those are the ones you have bled
I'm sure there's a Commandment on stealing something ignored by a few
And the rape of women and children is something some Christians will do

There's one that mentions no killing; quickly ignored at a test
As you suddenly notice their failings; no sin when it's simply a pest
You've an out when praying in temples for you worship all manner of things
Gold, jewels and objects greed of which others may sing

It was mentioned about bearing false Witness an art many lawyer will do
Distorting the truth for a client when honesty may offer a clue
It's two thousand years since Jesus, the Tablets were written BC
As peoples who follow the Commandments, so, why is Donald still free?

INUIT PAIN

My three generations of sisters
have been abused by a man not known
A statistic among Native women
this pain is never out-grown
Kayla was six when it started
when she sat in the lap of a man
A psychologist said talk to a policeman
her File is now buried in sand

Meta took a drink at a party
but the boys thought she was keen
Took it in turns through her agony
her life now blighted by dream
Marie never got over her moment
men queued at her door every day
Drink the only salvation
till she chased the devils away

Ebony was watching a TV court-case
when memories came back in a blast
A terrible day she had hidden
drugged and abused in her past
These crimes are not rare in Alaska
A fact ignored by the Law
It's breaking the heart of us Natives
why do they say we're the flaw

There's been FIFTY here in this courtroom
each girl abused and in pain
Why does this happen in Anchorage
Our State with a terrible stain

OUR LOST CHILDREN OF ISRAEL

Where are they now our lost children of Israel
stole from us parents because we were poor
tent living nomads of Morocco and Yemen
from Egyptian wastes and the lands of the Moor

We ran from the Atlas and lonely Sahara
fought to exist; for we heard of this Land
fled from the tribes of distant Arabia
then to discover some of us banned

For thousands of years we had lived in the desert
kept pure in our heart Torah and God
who are strangers preachers of Zionism
hatred of others not sparing the rod

Where are our children, where have they gone to
why did you take them, please tell us why?
seventy long years without an answer
each day of pain we parents cry

SOUTH ON THE BORDER DOWN MEXICO WAY

There's a shadow hanging over the Border
yet it's not the wall of Trump
but the tortured bodies of peoples
lying out in the Stump
Refugees escaping from poverty,
violence, extortion back home
hoping for a chance to live better
while avoiding the US Guards who roam

When caught they're often beaten
simply for pleasure it seems
kicked, punched tasered
enjoyment the pleasure of screams
evidence wiped by whispers
protected by Seniors in power
sand hides the body from vultures
cactus and innocent flower
Wives and children are wailing
pleading for the Body they know
Husband, brother is missing
sure that they heard the last blow

Entrenched in the psyche of this Border
emblematic the pattern they see
They're chaff for the Boots to trample,
these Guards who murder for free.
Let's rid this Border of vermin
two-legged rats of this kind
who see themselves as elitist
ignoring the poor being blind
Legislate these creatures to prison
all given a similar trial
Let us see these guards laughing
they're all in denial!!

THE WHITE HOUSE

A Reporter asked if I'd check out a story this story that old men did tell
about nightmares they had since children had they lived in a place worse than Hell
It had got to the ears of the Governor an Inquiry was held right away
No evidence found said the Governor, no bodies were found in the clay

One Mam doubted this Statement, refused to believe how her Son died
Pneumonia so soon after arrival; was sure the Authorities had lied
As a Forensic Scientist I dig up bodies Corpses that were hid in the ground
People who'd been killed at some terrible time; hidden where not to be found

MARIANNA a small town in Florida with a Reform School where
bad boys would go
Where the Bad was really the Teachers? Had they buried those boys in a row?
In a Graveyard was marked four crosses, but I found no bodies inside
So I scanned all around that meadow and discovered that many had died

A White house stood alone from the buildings. Death seemed to be oozing from it
With a lever I opened the padlock, then scanned the walls with my kit.
There was blood everywhere on the woodwork gore soaked into the wall
Tissue and skin under my feet all human from children quite small

In that room stood a strange contraption powered by motor and belt
It was a thrashing machine for those children what horror and terror each felt
Let there be no Court or Trial with a Lawyer they'd quickly be free
Let it beat them to death with this paddle, its disgust was eating at me

The School had been run as a factory where the Boys harvested the crop
Locals had been lining their pockets no one knew when to stop

Opened 1900 – Closed in 2011 to be sold in a property deal to locals.
In 2019 Dr. Erin Kimmerle forensic scientist found 55 graves, the investigation continues
This was done in the 'Bible Belt' by God-fearing folks!

THE VETERAN'S PRAYER

Heh man can you tell me where have I gone wrong?
I've done what you commanded I've done my Desert Storm
I've suffered wounds in Vietnam, lost limbs and bits of mind
Heh man can you tell me why I am doing time?
Yeah wars are long forgotten when YOU think the time is right
Words not writ in history or tamed with lack of bite
The loss of friend or buddy for me so hard to bear
to you a distant number from millions more to spare

I've dropped by stick in foreign lands, or choppered battle-zones
Tree jumped in Malaya, suffered breaking bones
Rotted flesh in jungles, eaten grass and rat
In Arctic wastes I've fought for you but it's help at home I lack!
You've filled us full of chemicals to fight the threat of gas
Bubonic plague to wild dog bites each soldier-boy must pass
You've lined us up to watch the bomb and see its blinding light
We must act in blind obedience as YOUR 'Powers That Be' are right

We've lost limbs, sight and touch, our bodies racked in pain
Suffered from the sights we've seen, doubted we were sane
But you argue the harm your drugs did that caused our 'Desert Storm'
Atomic flash that caused our ills since sixty years have gone
You bring us home in body bags, Paraded for the 'Flag'
Us scarred and tissue samples, lack a medal tag
Hidden in some hospital or dumped upon a street
Incapacity not an issue where politicians rarely meet

Yes our Country needs us when we're fighting for the Cause
Killing in some far off land some tribe who've not our flaws
"Wait, it's over Budget" or "The Elected want us out"
And it's "Let's get out of here! You soldiers, work it out!
Hide the badly wounded, forget the body count,
Smile to the media then quickly tiptoe out."

CANADIANS THE PACIFIED PEOPLES

Since the day that you arrived you've manipulated and lied
Broke every Treaty that's been signed
Twisted every fact with Laws that you enact
Our Peoples the ones you have fined
You've stolen any land by force or under-hand
Reserved us to ground that's bleak and poor
Our bison have been murdered, while children have been plundered
for conversion to your Religion as a cure

Our Customs have been banned by a Legislative band
to wipe any history from our mind
No Sweat Lodge or Sun Dance we will ever get the chance
for attempting to do so has us fined
Then you took our youth to school to a God of iron rule
to beat any Indian out their head
They were taken by Police any contact it would cease
Learning scripture often daily it was said

Nothing could be worse but you produced another curse
to tear each child from Mother's arms
You sent each one away while our feet were filled with clay
for adoption off in distant lands
Our lands are raped for dust as you've eaten up its crust
Polluted lakes and rivers with your power
You've hollowed out our earth keeping nothing in reserve
as your future is that moment to the hour

Be it Canadian or Pacific, Australian: each distinctive
American or Siberian in your lust
From the Amazon to Arctic, you've been ruthless and tragic
Rare a single People you've not touched

SORRY

Why does it take so long to say sorry to you both? Why does it take so long?
I've broken your hearts all through these years and it's taken me far too long
You tried all you could to raise me so good, you tried with all that you knew
and for years I tried not once did I cry learning and growing with you

But first came the fags o what a drag hiding each breath from your kiss
roll ups or old dotes I'd hide in my coat or taking the pennies you'd miss
Then offered a pill the latest to thrill ecstasy addiction in form
free at the gate from a boy who was late dare I, would I, conform?

Now I've tried all the rest, some of the best, never a care for my life
cocaine for tea, hashish all free, never a thought for your strife
How mother coped while I laughed and joked; ignored all the words that she said
of the tears that you lost at what terrible cost all flew over my head

With my septum all gone eaten or worn needle tracks on my arms and my thighs
My partner is dead blown out of her head our youngest addicted to highs
What's money to me is a drop in the sea thousands I've snorted and shot
near died from the dabs of needles and jabs and the methadone treatment I've got

So leave me alone I'll never come home I've found my niche in the sewer
I've got this disease which will never please and I know there's no chance of a cure
O why has it taken so long to say sorry Daddy? Why has it taken so long?
I've broken your hearts all through these years and it's taken me far too long

PLEASE TELL US

In this Country of Britain after the War
you scattered us children, please tell us what for
At a time in our lives we thought the worst
A law was created; for us a real curse
Some had lost parents or their Mum couldn't cope
Us orphaned and lonely without any hope
You gathered us up and sent us away
Shipped to the Commonwealth, no chance we could stay
Us children just vanished gone for all time
Wiped from the records not even a sign

Some of us cried and wept when you came
Families were split and we kids were to blame
Not even the Jews were now without hope
We were destined for oblivion; it wasn't a joke
We landed in countries all very strange
Van Demiens Land or Canadian Range
Lost and alone, in need of a friend
We were given to folks what ever their trend

Some went to ones who were kind and were good
Most went to others who were up to no good
Treated like slaves, to do all the chores
Girls often beaten or treated like whores
Broken and bleeding, rare were we spared
A few would be murdered, nobody cared
Boys would be raped if there wasn't a girl
Men could do anything when they needed a thrill

Where could we run to, where could we go
Nowhere to hide, escape just a no
So we've grew up with anger inside
Pleading for help, always denied
We've hunted for brothers or sisters we had
Appealed to the Media, some thought us mad
Got help from the telly at least for a while
They hunted for us, they searched with great guile

Some folks were lucky they found the match
Screened around Christmas for viewers to catch
But most of us now live without any hope
Compensation now... it's only a joke

DUNAVERTY

Bloody was that rock on that wild Kintyre shore
Bloody was that rock by the sea
Murder under a white flag shown
On the rock of Dunaverty

When we were children we played in its shadow
Pail and spade at the water's edge
Never did we know of its tragic secrets
While hunting for crabs by a rocky ledge

Retreated in vain to hide in their castle
Chased by an army with murder in mind
Trusting they were safe in that seashore fortress
Not from an army whose lust was blind

Often we climbed on its grassy slopes
Feeling that moment of breeze on our face
Searching the beach as true knights of conquest
Dreams of the past were often the case

Offering the flag after three days of siege
Expecting their leaders to die by the sword
Yielding to promises quickly given
Died to a man with the words of Our Lord

If only we'd known of the murder and slaughter
Not even a child was allowed to survive
Locals were threatened to erase the memory
Not one to be seen with a tear in their eye

Bloody was the beach on that wild Kintyre shore
Bloody was that rock by the sea
Slaughter to a man in the name of the Lord
Died for the right to be free.

A GHOST OF A CHANCE

Oh it is terrible the pain I felt
by beatings I often received from the belt
For hours and days I cried in my room
No love did I feel, those walls were my tomb
For years I suffered this pain in my life
and attempted to end it by the edge of a knife
Torture within was the hardest to cope
it twisted my guts, my heart had no hope

      All through my life I've lived in Care
      often abused my soul lying bare
      Never did I hear an encouraging word
      Language spoken did only disturb
      So I grew up with this terrible life
      till drink and drugs completed my strife
      It was then that I sunk into a pit
      with life so black it was hit after hit

Then along came someone who handled me well;
Offered me hope as I stumbled and fell
Lifted me up gave chance to cope
with banter, support, sometimes a joke
And, gradually I climbed from that hole
still lived on the streets, yes lived like a mole

      Burrowing deep in those streets of the night
      hiding for places to shut out the light
      Begging for that chance to stay alive
      now I had hope I had to survive
      I grovelled, pleaded to be given the chance,
      to come out of the gutter try to advance
      Hold down a job no matter what,
      a few pence in hand, more often not

Yes I saved, and struggled to better myself
Washed off dirt, found clean dress
Maybe I looked like tramp in a field
I didn't have airs but each moment I'd feel
Then I lost touch with my Samaritan friend
I hunted and searched it seemed like the end
Once I remembered some words he'd say,
when he offered hope I might need to pay

Now I have escaped from those years of Hell
with kids of my own my story I'll tell
I'll forget all the bitterness I felt in those years,
give a cuddle to them, love when there's tears
And to some of the kids who live on the street
maybe one day someone kind you will meet
who will offer just then the gift of a glance
to give it once that Ghost of a Chance.

GOLDEN ANNIVERSARY

As told by an ex-POW survivor of WW2 Japan

Aye it's fifty years this Christmas thit she became ma wife
An despite awe oor trials an tribulations am glad wi met in life
Wi used-tae argi every day
An hur mates wid say that man yiv gote, wull sharely nivver stay

Wi hud four boe-ys, jist yin efter thi ither
Thi wur jist like peas in a pod, an each yin wis like thir mither
An things wur fine fur us until thi reached intae thur teens
Life fur us taen a bad turn whin thi lived ootside thur means

It started wae oor eldest smoking whin at skill
Wi didnae ken the half o it, it wiz drugs, an thae cun kill
He stole tae feed his habit, taen money frae hur purse
A cannae tell yi thi things he'd dae tae feed this awfy curse

Despite awe thir promises tae both me an thir Mam
His brithers jist followed him, thi didnae care a damn
Thid lie an cheat an rob an steal, tae shoot intae thir erm
Or sniff or pop or smoke thi stuff, thi didnae ken its herm

Within ten year wid lost three boe-ys, dea-in in despair
Overdosed wi heroin, fur us it wisnae fair
Thi youngest, he screwed thi heed fir a few mair years at least
An settled doon, hud a faemly, wi thocht he'd tamed thi beast

He hud three wee girls ages ten tae fowr
Wi used tae go-an visit, thid meet us at thi door
Wi felt right prood whin wi saw thim, thocht things wur gettin richt
An thim weans wid gae us drawins wi thocht thi wur quait bricht

It wis whin thi youngest saed shi'd a new Granny, wi thocht it kin a strange
Wi listened tae whit thi bairn said an A flew intae a rage
Thir new Granny an Grandpa wur thi folks that lived next door
Thi Granny fed ma boe-y wi drugs, wi this a felt sae sore

But hur man, he wiz thi Bastard, tae gae himsell some thrills
Abused oor pair wee grandweans, abused thae little girls
Wi go-at thi Polis, thi Social workers too
Thae took thae bairns intae Care wi rarely see thim noo

An noo wiv lost oor youngest, he disnae want tae know
Wi thought this wid be thi last straw, oor final body blow
But God can be right cruel whin he sees yir really doon
Whin yir settled in yir bubble, he'll nip yir wee balloon

A lost ma leg tae gangrene an Mam huz lost hur sicht
But we'll celebrate oor special day this comin Christmas nicht.

CLIMB

At mists of dawn we set to climb through jewelled grass
and sweet bruised thyme
among the slabs of fallen rock from cliffs on high, in time forgot
Racing on with heaving breath, sweating streaks, no time for rest
until amid its base we mull and brew, study route, take in the view
A trail of breeze in jetstream cloud, a patchwork quilt of greens and browns
Below see ants, in truck and car; the rising sun now clear and high
Unpack each sack of rope and gear, tensions loose in secret fear
Clip on crab and brothers light, into harness neat and tight

Belt in loop then turn it back, on with helmet buckle strap
Shake the rope to see it run, hitch on knot to each in turn
Jim there will take the lead, while I stand and need to heed
his route, to scale by foot and hand, the way on cliff we both had planned
With left foot neat and into crack, fingers feel for groove face mark
right leg stretch then heel on ledge, hand now grips in tightened wedge
spider-like on rock face wall legs askew then standing tall
fingers hunt by tip for hole and stretch to seek their goal

Belayed set then distant call. Taken strain I strive on wall
on hidden steps, from place to place gathering secrets as I trace
pitch by pitch ever on fingers numbed, rubbed and gone
Lead to lead stretch ever up a moments fear a chance of luck
Ice-like fangs now greet our eye by crampon feet we kick and try
Swing axe swing and hammer blow onwards upwards steady slow
piton, screw, or trusted friend crabbed and locked, secured rope end
Guided on by patient hands across the face of layered band

Howling wind and spindrift blows sugared ice and powdered snows
swirling windspouts, daggered pain needle hail by demon rain
Goggled eyes all blue or pink peer through sheets of fiery zinc
Breath of frost adhered to beard; crumpled step each kick is feared
Rope now stiff, all kink and bend upwards steady never end
up through chimney legs a-splay dangled axe all hoar and grey
Ten foot, nine foot, then outcrop a final heave to bridge the top

In blast and stagger, hug and grin as screaming banshees, howling wind
Descend, descend, rappel as quick with bated breath, controlled and slick
Compass poised in sure direction a moments lack; a sick infection
Giddy grinning full of hope, stumbling shuffling, icy slope
Find a lee to check the mark, wanderlust in white-out stark
Fear returns in stomach screw, Indian-file lead and queue
Balling snow on easing slope inch by inch in downward grope
Frozen cheeks in Viking face, blocks of snow in rippled race
Crack then slide in fearsome roll with eddied rush to feed its soul

Crampons off stacked on sack, rope in loops, bent and cracked
Holstered both, hammer, axe. Onwards now on homeward tracks
back to pub forgotten pain slaked our need for it again
Fingers, toes, nipped survive but, *atop the climb supreme alive!*

THE WRENs

As I sit on this rock just by the shore
I remember that day so long ago
We'd been posted here just after the War
to let us heal from that poisonous sore

It certainly was a glorious day
when we went to this beach
to relax and play
As soon as we could we went for a swim
some stripped down naked and went straight in

Desperate to shed the stench of blood
to cleanse ourselves with that endless flood
No signs we saw on this deserted beach
of that Danger warning just out of reach

And it looked for all the world to see
a piece of Highland tranquillity
Atlantic rollers, a place to play
in warmth and sun – we'd stay all day

But as the giant waves crashed asunder
fearsome rip-tides sucked them under
pulling my four friends into deadly quicksand
Katherine and Maggie and Doris and Ann

Yes as we laughed and played they drowned
in liquid sand not solid ground
and I know we'd lost good friends in the War
in amongst all that blood and gore

We really thought we'd escaped all that
in this place of heaven he'd sprung his trap
Oh! I stayed on in this part of Kintyre
and married, yes married a local man

And every day I come here to see
if my friends I lost will return from the sea
and if Katherine and Maggie and Doris and Ann
will escape from the clutches of that evil quicksand

Isn't it strange
when one tells the truth

that the Media
consider it quite obtuse
as

within the minds
of Editors and Press

they aim each barb
to cause distress

Yiv red ma wirds
o noo an then
if yid laik sum mair
let mi ken

j1m2mcrobert@gmail.com

Ingram Content Group UK Ltd.
Milton Keynes UK
UKHW020632240523
422260UK00005B/164